SAMPSON
THE HOT TUB BEAR
a true story

BY WENDY TOKUDA

ILLUSTRATED BY LOKKEN MILLIS

ROBERTS RINEHART PUBLISHERS
Boulder, Colorado

To My Family
Richard, Mikka, and Maggie Hall
—WT

To David, Natalie, and Leah,
the finest people in my life
—LM

Special thanks to Connie and Gary Potter, Forrest deSpain
and the Orange County Zoo, and KACTV

Published by
ROBERTS RINEHART PUBLISHERS
6309 Monarch Park Place
Niwot, Colorado 80503

Distributed to the trade by Publishers Group West

Published in the UK and Ireland by
ROBERTS RINEHART PUBLISHERS
Trinity House, Charleston Road
Dublin 6, Ireland

Project editor: *Betsy Armstrong*
Art direction, cover design: *Ann W. Douden*
Design & production: *Polly Christensen*

10 9 8 7 6 5 4 3 2 1

Printed in Hong Kong through Phoenix Offset

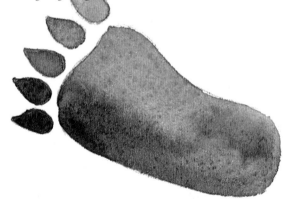

International Standard Book Number 1-57098-090-X

Library of Congress Cataloging-in-Publication data

Tokuda, Wendy.
    Samson the hot tub bear: a true story / by Wendy Tokuda;
illustrated by Lokken Millis.
        p.   cm.
    Summary: When a large cinnamon bear was found eating and
swimming in residential backyards in Monrovia, California, he was
captured in order to be put to death, but through the efforts of some
of the people he had visited he was spared and moved to a zoo instead.
    ISBN 1-57098-209-0 (HC)
    1 Samson (Bear)—Juvenile literature.   [1. Samson (Bear)
    2. Bears.]   I. Millis, Lokken. ill.   II. Title.
    QL737.C27T65   1998
    599.78'092'9–dc21
    [B]   97-47295
                                         CIP
                                         AC

Prologue

Samson the bear was a frequent visitor in the small town of Monrovia, California, during the summer of 1994. The 400-pound, cinnamon-colored bear became known as the "hot tub bear" because he loved Jacuzzis. He was also fond of the avocados and other fruits that grew in neighborhood yards.

Eventually, Samson got in trouble with the law for raiding garbage cans, destroying fruit trees, peering into windows, walking through backyards, and generally living the good life.

Samson was captured on September 18, 1994, and scheduled to be put to sleep the very next day. But the old bear became an overnight cause célèbre after Connie and Gary Potter's videos of Samson lounging in their hot tub were shown on national television news.

Just two hours before Samson was scheduled to die, Governor Pete Wilson gave him a stay of execution.

Using donations and volunteer help, the Orange County Zoo in Irvine built a new enclosure just for the hot tub bear— swimming pool, waterfall and all.

After five months in a temporary holding facility, Samson was welcomed into his new home in February 1996. He is still living there today.

Every evening in the late summer,
just as the stars began to appear in the sky,
Samson the bear lumbered down out of the quiet hills
to look for dinner.

Samson knew exactly where to find his favorite foods.
Wonderful foods like avocados, dates, and figs!

And then there was garbage.
Samson loved garbage.

One evening, Samson discovered a swimming pool
where he could take a little dip and cool off.

Next to the pool was a hot tub.
Every night, Samson soaked in
the warm, steamy water and relaxed.

Afterward, he would pad over to the lawn
and roll on his back. He'd scratch his stomach
with his huge paw, and gaze out at
the twinkling lights of the city.

Sometimes, as Samson walked across the patio,
he saw a man and a woman in the window.
But people didn't scare Samson.
They didn't bother him, and he didn't bother them.

Connie and Gary Potter were terrified
the first time they saw the old bear through the window.
But soon they began to look forward to his nightly visits.

Samson never made a sound as he approached
through the bushes. Whenever the Potters
heard a big splash, they would hurry to the
window. Their hearts pounding, they videotaped
the huge bear lounging in their pool and Jacuzzi,
as if he were on holiday.

One night, Samson ate some garbage that made him very sick.
The Potters watched and worried as Samson rolled
on their lawn in pain.

They called the fish and game wardens for help.
They would know what to do!

Well, the game wardens knew all about
the old bear. They'd been hearing complaints
for months about a cinnamon bear that
had ruined fruit trees, knocked down fences,
spilled garbage and scared people half to death
by peering in their windows.

They worried that someone might get hurt.

Samson's stomach got better on its own, but his problems
were just beginning.

Now that the wardens knew his favorite hangout,
they put out a big trap baited with food.
Within a few days, Samson was caught.

Right away, the wardens saw that he was an old bear—
he had hardly any teeth left! What could they do with him?

If they moved him farther into the mountains he would
just come back. No zoos wanted him, because they all
had plenty of black bears.

So, Samson would have to be put to sleep.
That's a polite way of saying he'd have
to be killed. And it would happen
quickly—the very next day.

The Potters were horrified!

If there was a way to save Samson's life,
they would have to move fast.

They rushed the videos of Samson lounging
in their hot tub to television news reporters.
Maybe, just maybe, someone, somewhere could help.

All this time, old Samson sat inside the dark trap—
cold, frightened, and alone.

The clock was ticking away.

That very night at 6:00 P.M., Samson would be put to sleep.

Just hours before Samson was to die, pictures of him relaxing
in the hot tub were shown on television news.
Immediately the phones started ringing.

Wasn't there some way to save the bear,
people wanted to know?

"He was just being a bear." someone said.
"And don't forget, the bears were here
before we were!"

Finally, all those voices reached the one person who could save Samson—the Governor of the State of California. His phones rang, and letters poured out of his fax machine.

Everyone seemed to love the old bear,
the Governor thought. Surely a home
could be found for Samson somewhere.

The Governor made a decision.
"Save the bear," he said.

Samson was saved! But he still had
no place to live.

The old bear was loaded onto a truck,
and driven for hours to a place
outside of Sacramento. Until he had
a home of his own, he would live
in a cement pen, enclosed by a
chain-link fence.

Samson hid inside his den, frightened by the sounds
of the reporters and cameras outside. For three days,
he wouldn't come out.

Finally, his caretaker lured him out with a trail of M&Ms.
Samson gobbled them up hungrily, and came outside
into the light.

From that day on, he adjusted quickly to life in captivity.

Food was always the main thing on his mind.
And he loved water. Old Samson would climb
right into his big tub of drinking water to cool off.
He was so big that when he squeezed in, almost
all the water spilled out onto the floor.

His handlers would hear a great splash and laugh.
"Samson is in the trough again."

Many months passed. Finally, a tiny zoo
in Southern California volunteered to give
Samson a permanent home. The zoo
took in a lot of wild animals no one else
wanted—including owls, raccoons,
and a bobcat. It volunteered to build
a new enclosure just for the hot tub bear.

Samson would be the biggest animal
in the zoo. No question about it—
he would be the star.

There was one problem, though. The little zoo
had no money to build the bear's enclosure.
So Samson's friends came to the rescue.
Connie and Gary sold postcards and posters
with Samson's picture. Children collected money.

A concrete company donated cement. The zoo director himself designed the enclosure and spent hours digging and painting.

People who saw Samson on TV came to help.

And one company even donated a pool and waterfall for the hot tub bear!

One day, after months in his tiny cell, old Samson
followed a trail of food right into a trailer.
There was more food inside, so he settled in
quietly and off he went for another long ride.
When the truck finally stopped, Samson was put
in a small cage to spend the night.

The next morning, the steel door on the cage lifted,
and the old bear ran outside. There was grass, and trees,
and fresh air—and his own pool with a waterfall!
Immediately he went for a swim. Samson was in his
new home at last.

More than a thousand people were there to welcome him,
including his old friends, the Potters. Children sang
a song written just for him. News cameras were everywhere.
Even the Governor came.

Love is a very powerful thing, and
nothing proves that more than the story
of the old bear named Samson.